MARVEL

ULTIMATE VILLAINS

Written by Cefn Ridout

Penguin
Random
House

Editorial Assistant Natalie Edwards
Project Art Editor Jon Hall
Project Editor Ruth Amos
Pre-production Producer Marc Staples
Senior Producer Mary Slater
Managing Editor Sadie Smith
Managing Art Editor Vicky Short
Publisher Julie Ferris
Art Director Lisa Lanzarini
Publishing Director Simon Beecroft

Reading Consultant Linda B. Gambrell, Ph.D

First American Edition, 2018
Published in the United States by DK Publishing
345 Hudson Street, New York, New York 10014

Page design copyright © 2018 Dorling Kindersley Limited
DK, a Division of Penguin Random House LLC

18 19 20 21 22 10 9 8 7 6 5 4 3 2 1
001–305863–April/2018

marvel.com
© 2018 MARVEL

Published in Great Britain by Dorling Kindersley Limited.

A catalog record for this book
is available from the Library of Congress.

ISBN: 978-1-4654-6684-6 (Paperback)
ISBN: 978-1-4654-6685-3 (Hardcover)

DK books are available at special discounts when purchased in bulk for
sales promotions, premiums, fund-raising, or educational use. For details, contact:
DK Publishing Special Markets, 345 Hudson Street, New York, New York 10014
SpecialSales@dk.com

Printed and bound in China

A WORLD OF IDEAS:
SEE ALL THERE IS TO KNOW

www.dk.com

Contents

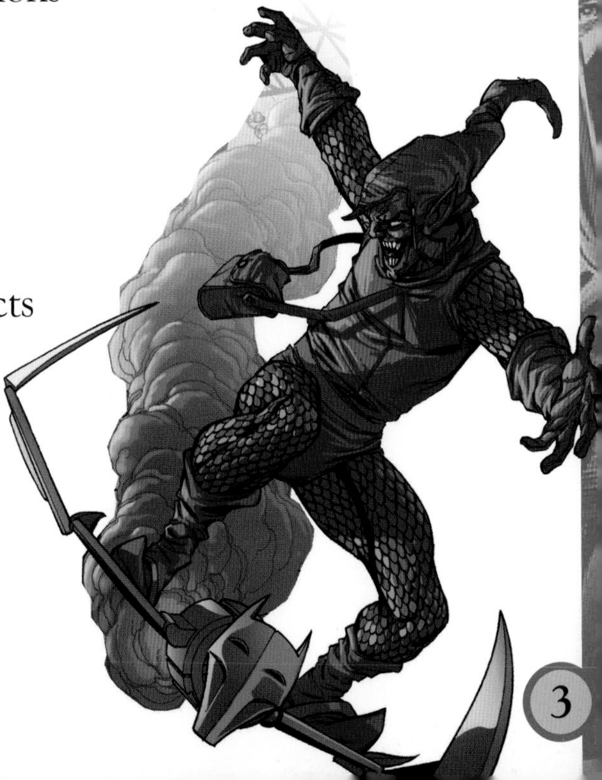

Fiendish villains

The universe is full of cunning, fearsome Super Villains. These criminals have awesome abilities and use amazing technology.

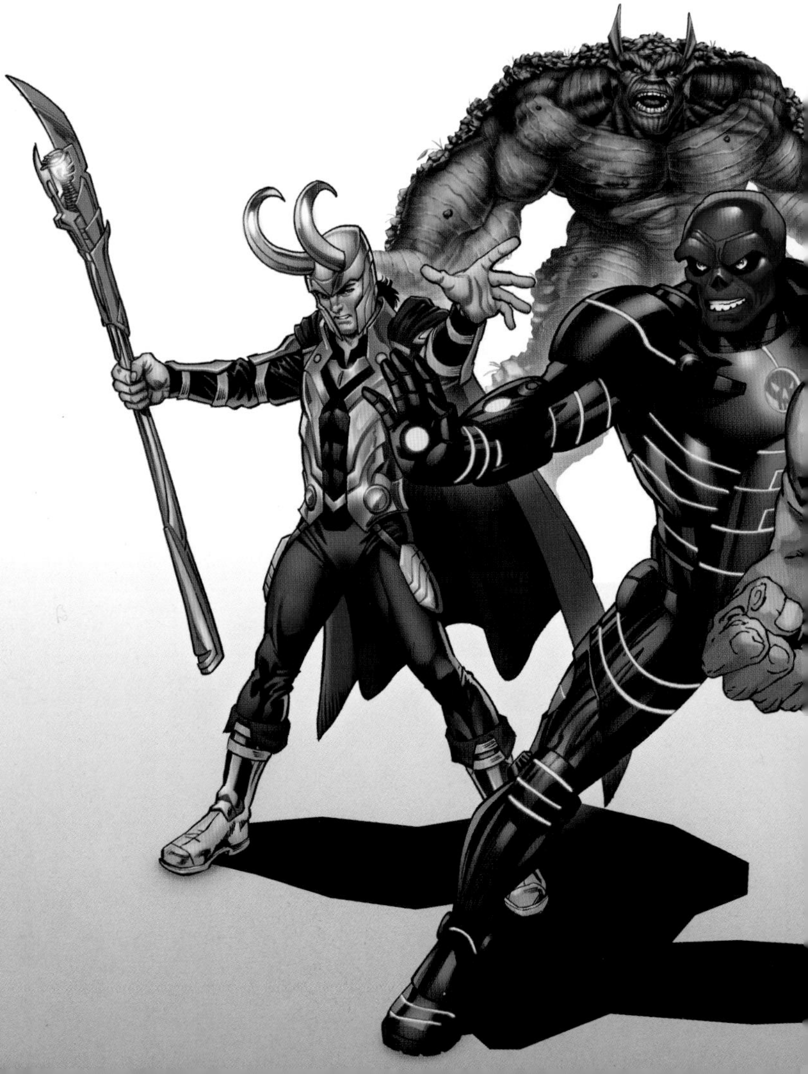

They are always planning evil schemes to get more power. Ultimate villains have Super Hero archenemies, who try to stop them from taking over the world!

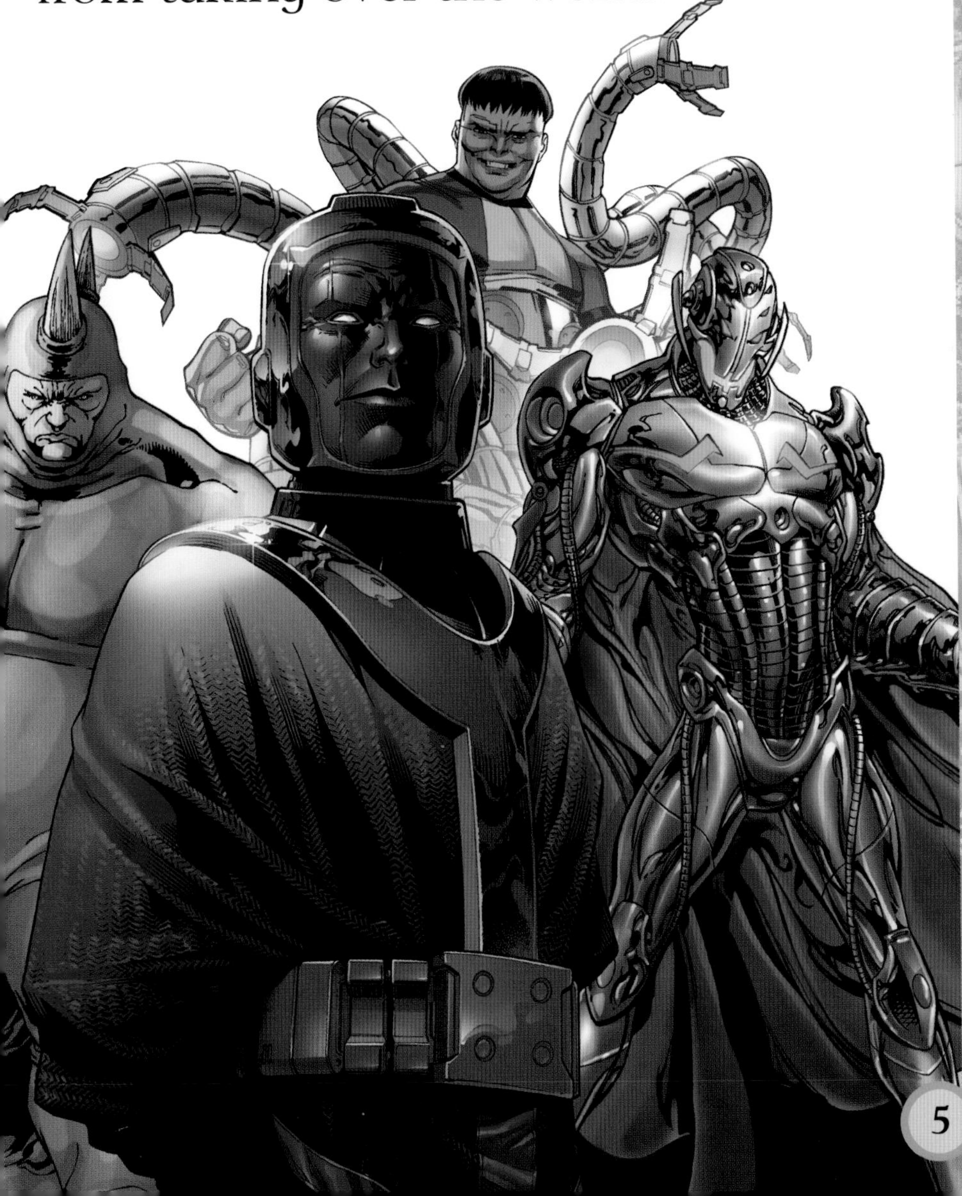

Thanos

Thanos is the ultimate bad guy.
He was born on Saturn's moon, Titan

Thanos is a sly and cruel villain.
He has a great deal of power,
and is determined to rule the galaxy.
Thanos will destroy anyone
who stands in his way!

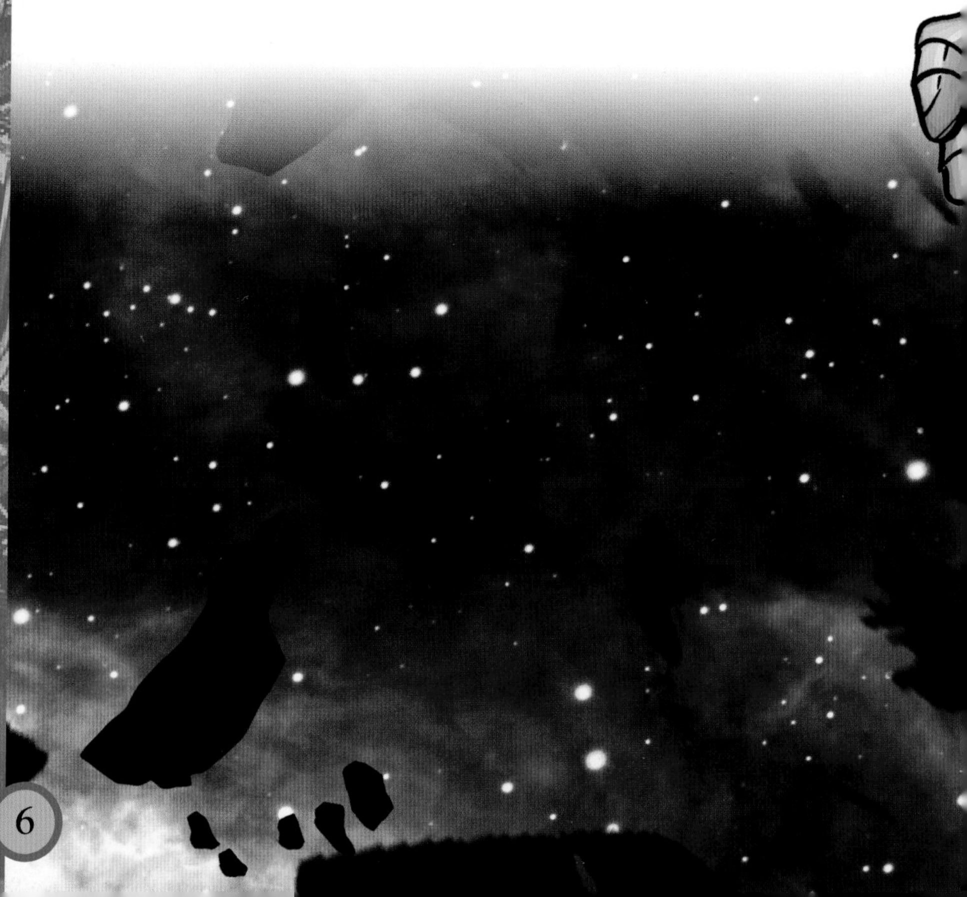

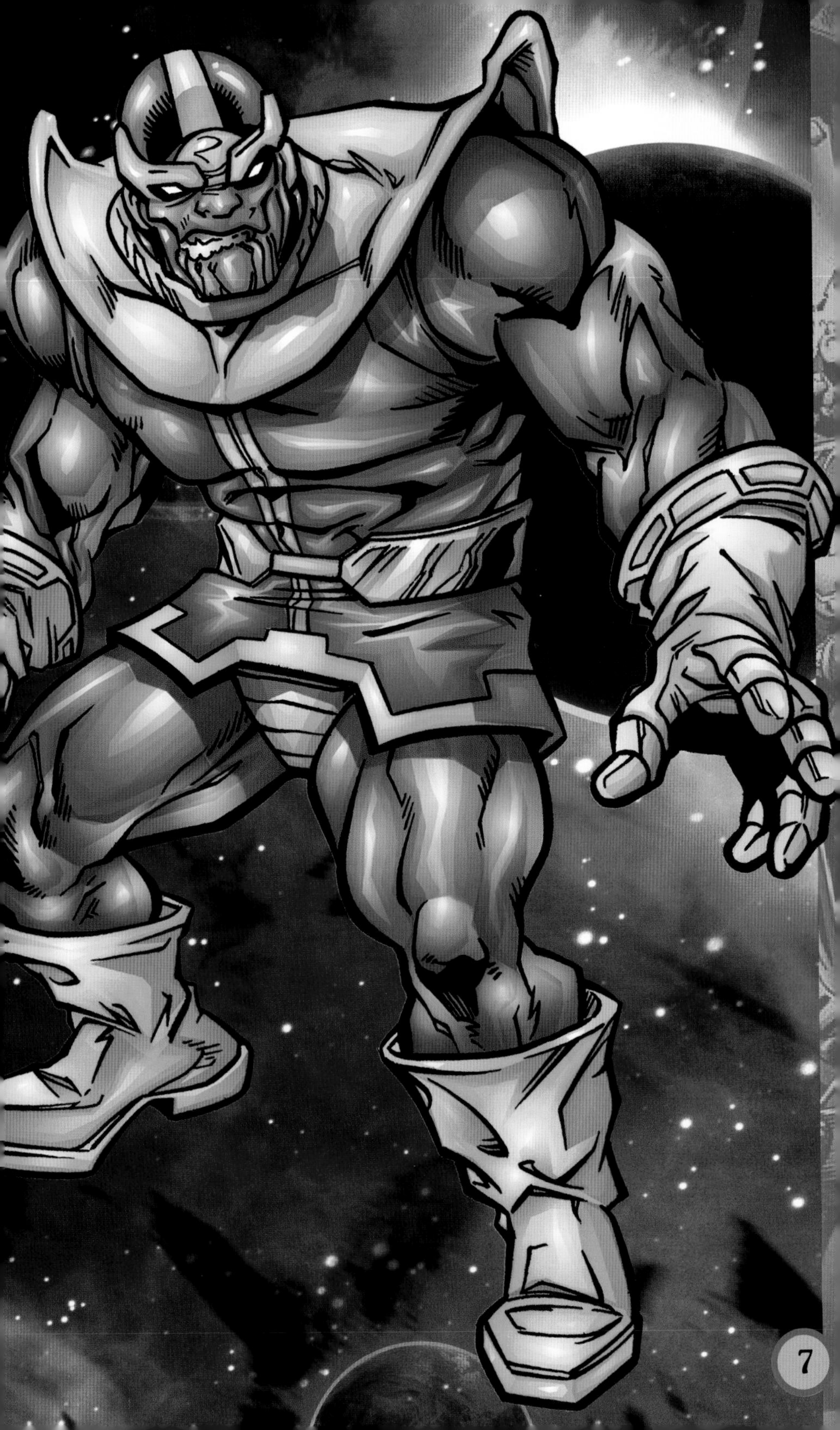

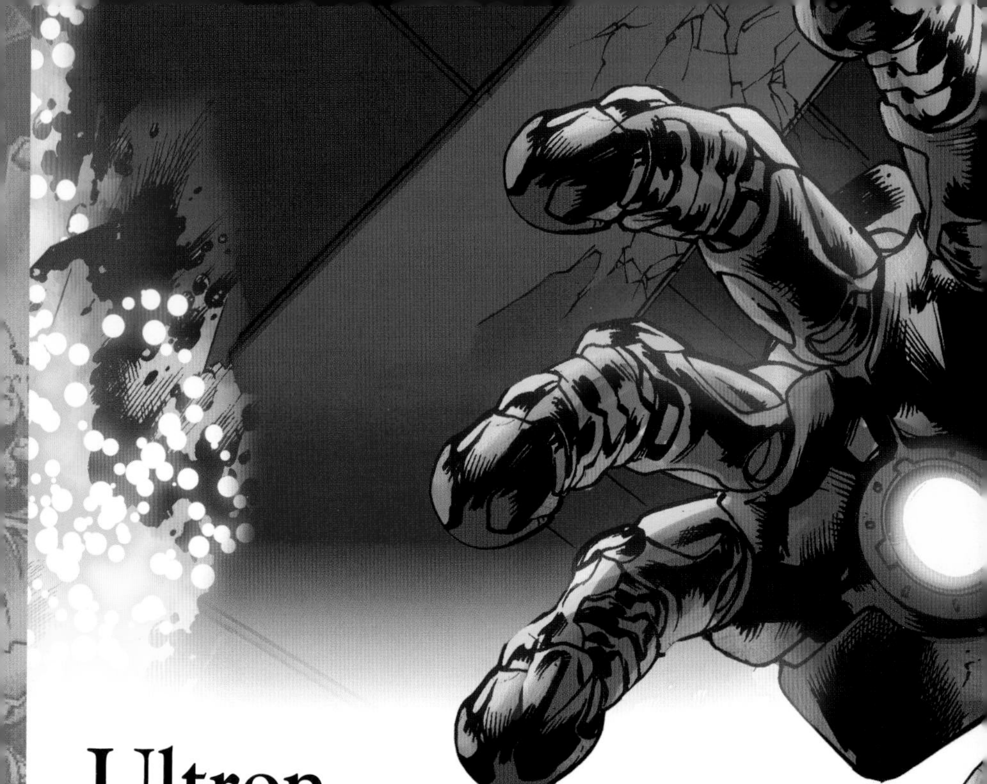

Ultron

Ultron is a wicked robot. He hates humans and is very intelligent. Ultron battles the Super Hero team the Avengers. He is one of their greatest enemies.

Every time Ultron is destroyed, he rebuilds himself to be deadlier than before. This robot is unstoppable!

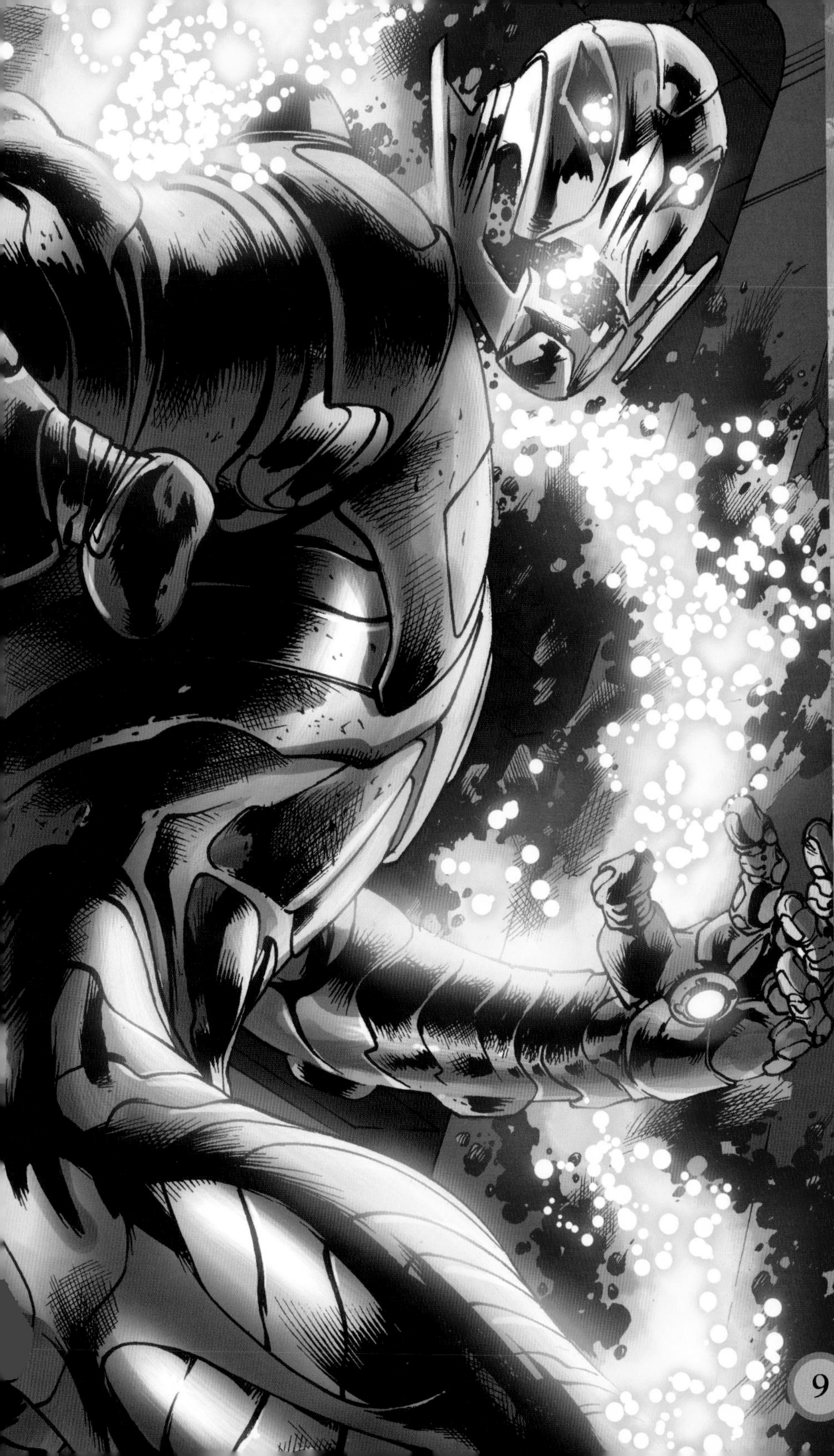

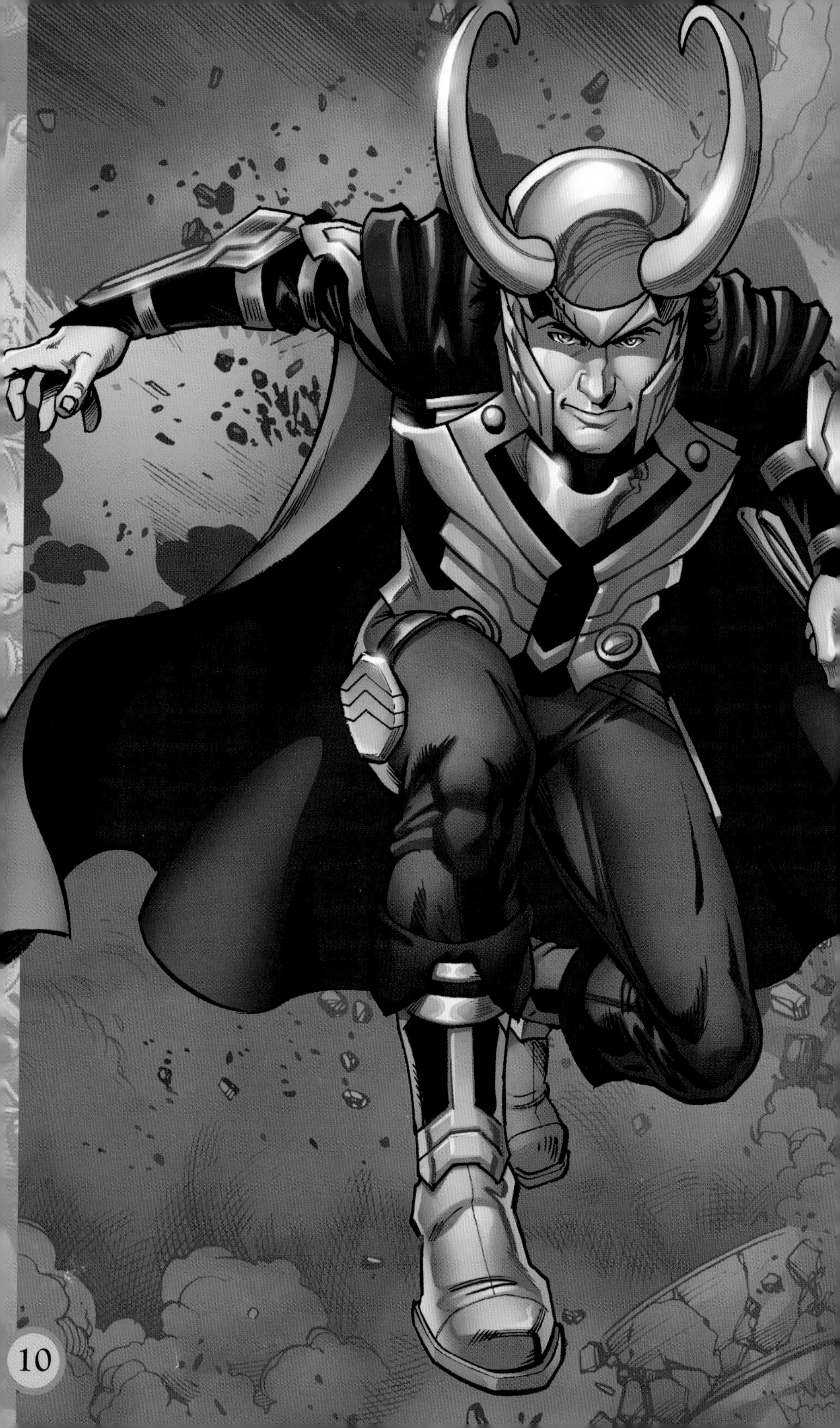

Loki

Loki is the God of Mischief.
He is the evil brother of the
Thunder God, Thor. He lives in
the magical kingdom of Asgard.

Loki can shape-shift
into any form he chooses.
He uses black magic
to play tricks, and to cause
mayhem for the Avengers.

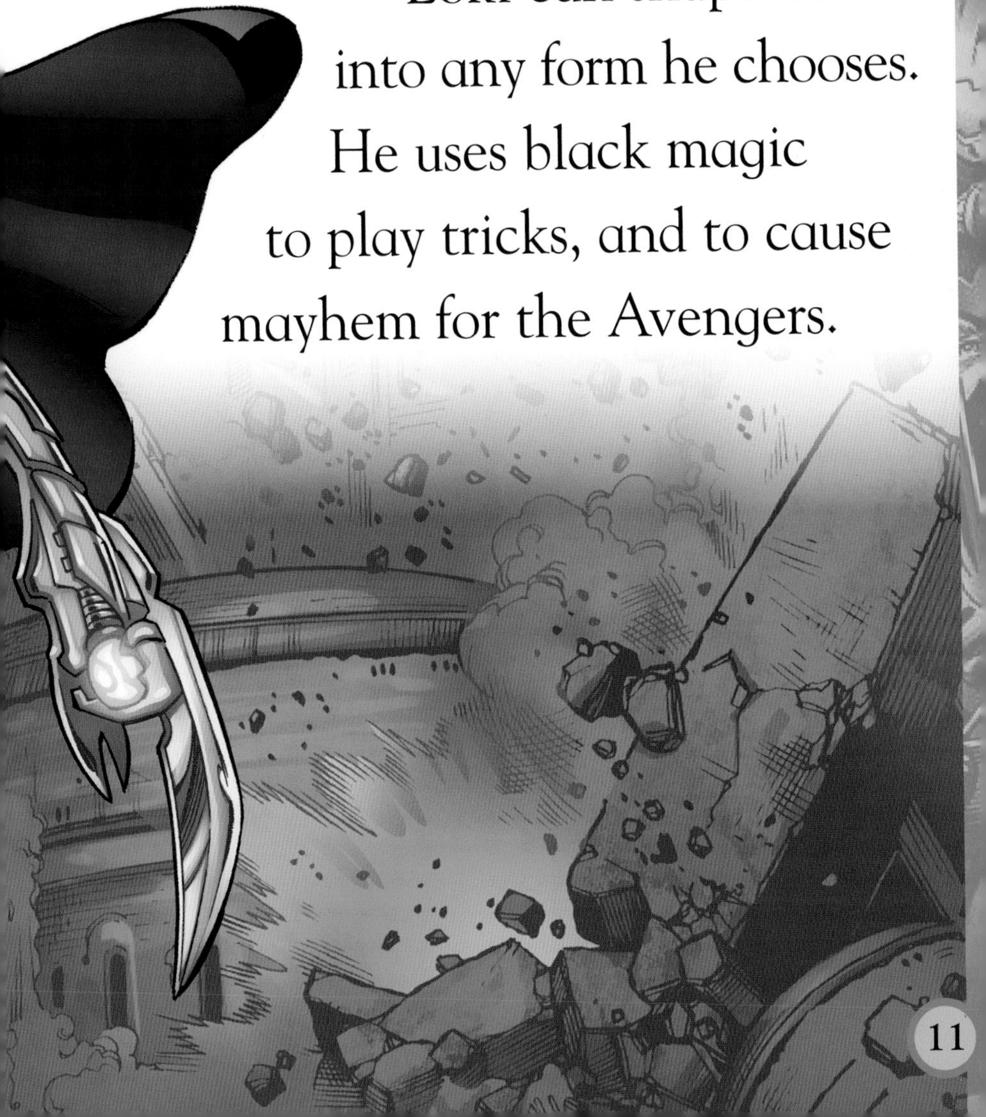

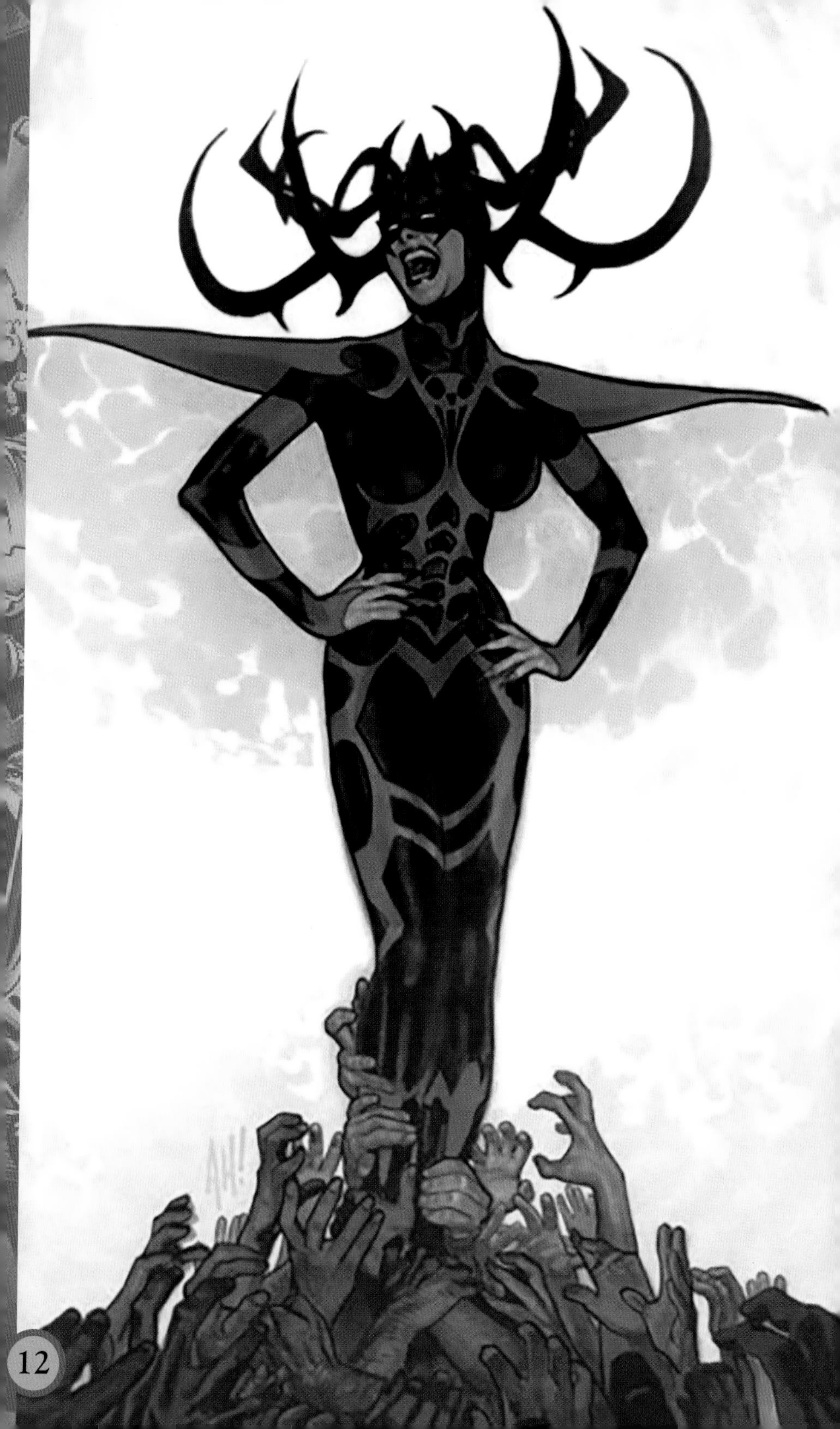
AH!

Hela

Hela is the Goddess of Death. She reigns over Hel, the creepy land of the dead. She wants to trap all gods and mortals in her cruel kingdom forever!

Hela has the power to kill with just one touch. The goddess also has a powerful weapon named Nightsword, but she prefers to use magic.

Doctor Octopus

Doctor Octopus has four menacing, mechanical tentacles. They became part of his body after an accident. He can move them using only his mind. His tentacles are super-strong.

Doctor Octopus is a brilliant scientist, but he is also a crook. He is a constant threat to the wall-climbing Super Hero Spider-Man, and to Spidey's family and friends.

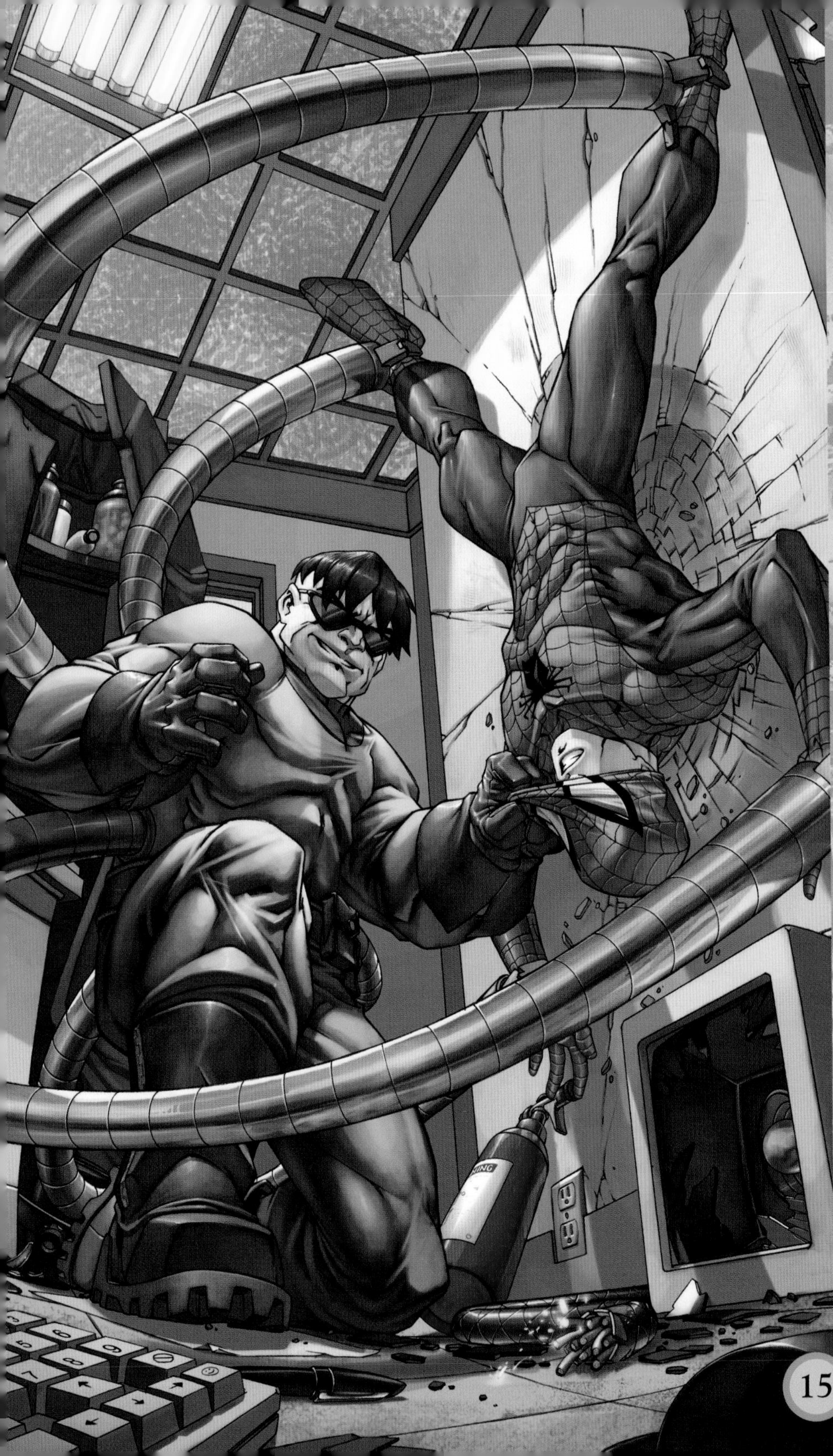

VILLAINOUS TEAMS

It isn't just heroes that form super-teams. Wicked villains join deadly groups, too. These criminals can conquer the universe with powerful allies by their sides!

Hydra

This evil organization of villains causes total chaos. Hydra uses secret agents to fight the Avengers.

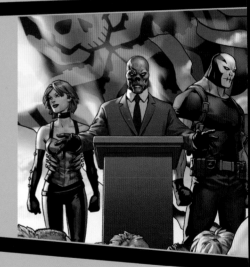

Sinister Six

Doctor Octopus set up this mean team to combat Spider-Man. Many members leave and join over time.

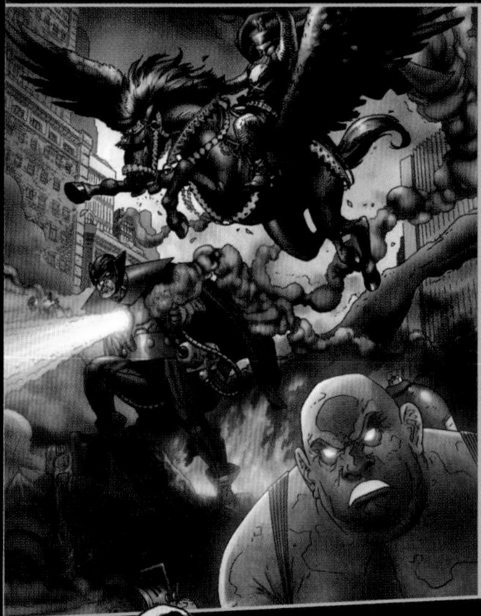

Masters of Evil

This criminal group was created in order to battle the Avengers. The Masters of Evil have lots of different powers and weapons.

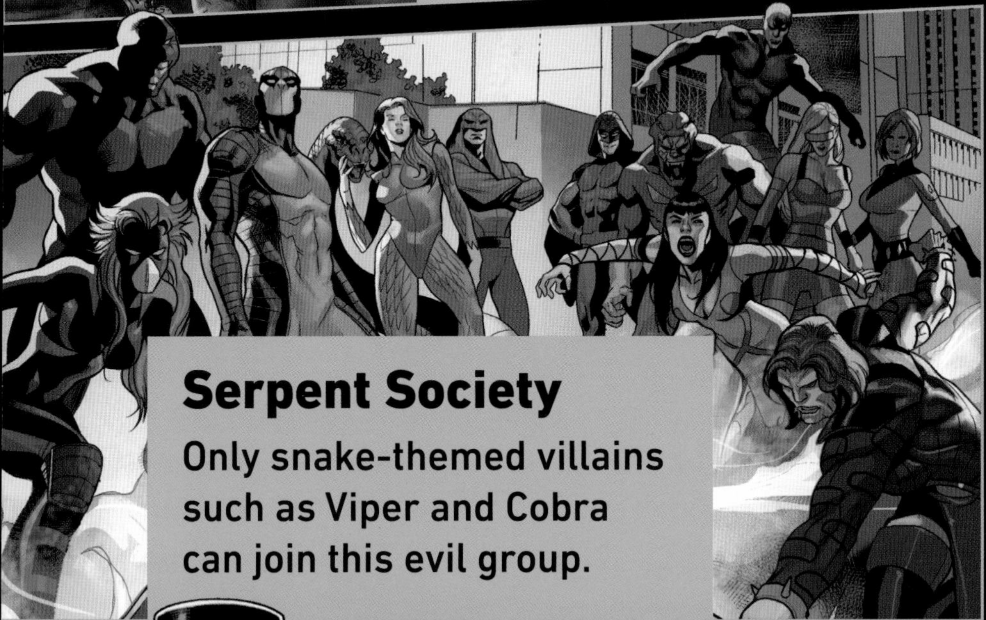

Serpent Society

Only snake-themed villains such as Viper and Cobra can join this evil group.

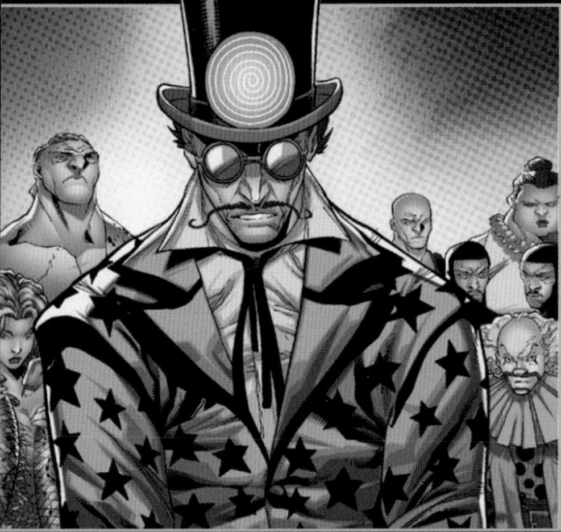

Circus of Crime

This team hypnotizes its audiences and steals from them during circus shows. The group fights heroes such as Hawkeye.

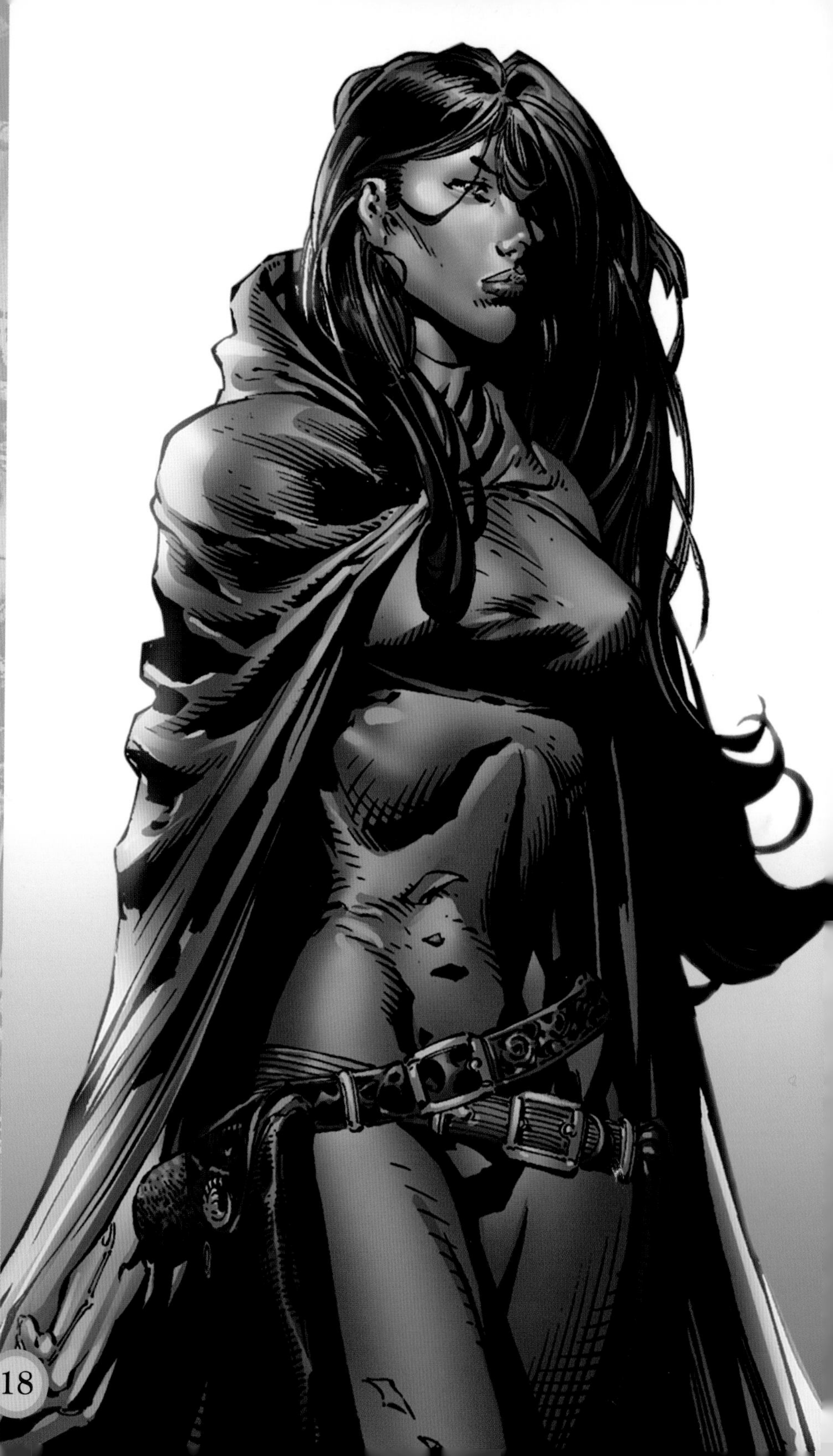

Madame Hydra

Madame Hydra trained as a spy before she became the leader of Hydra. This snake-themed villain is also known as Viper. She is the leader of the sneaky Serpent Society, too.

Madame Hydra's favorite weapon is poison. She uses poison darts, toxic lipstick, and her hollowed fangs to deliver deadly venom.

Red Skull

Red Skull is very wicked. He is so evil that even other Super Villains do not want to work with him.

Red Skull is able to transfer his mind into other people's bodies. This means he can live forever! The brave Super Hero Captain America finds it difficult to destroy him.

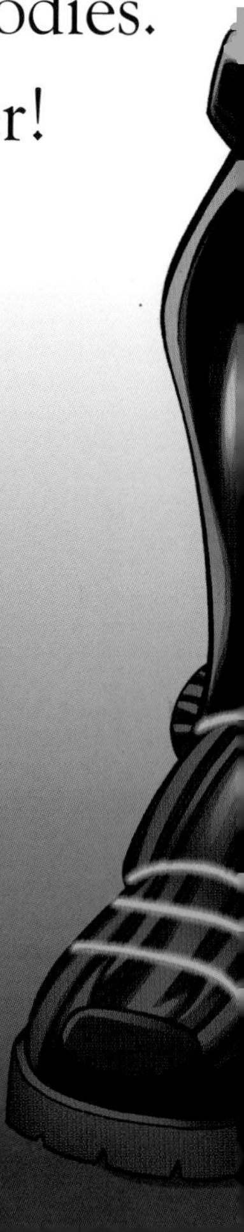

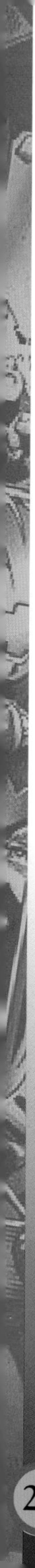

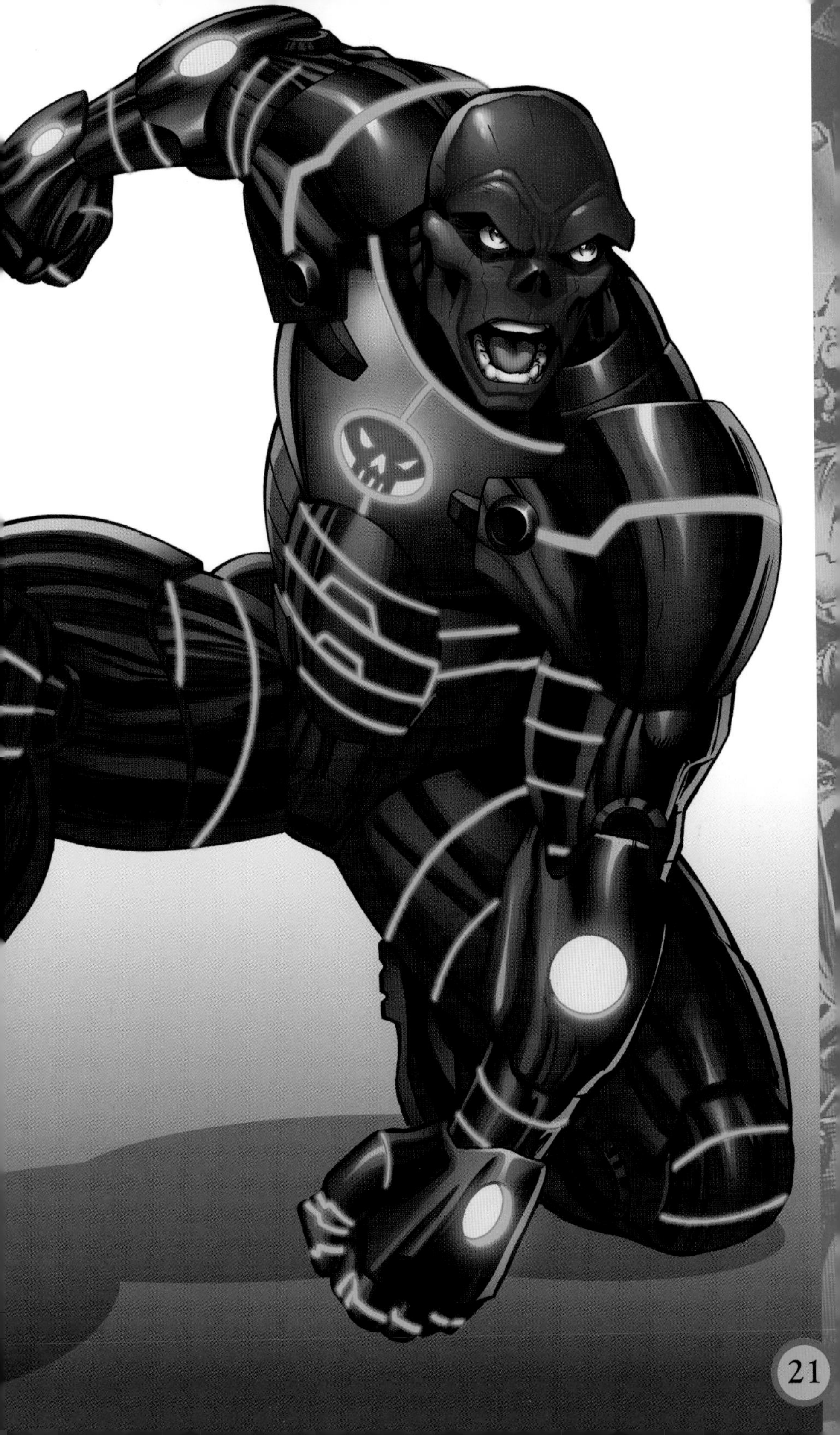

Green Goblin

Norman Osborn is the Green Goblin. He is mean and cunning. This Super Villain flies around New York on his Goblin Glider, causing trouble.

Green Goblin became a crime lord in order to take over the world. He also wants to crush the web-slinging Spider-Man!

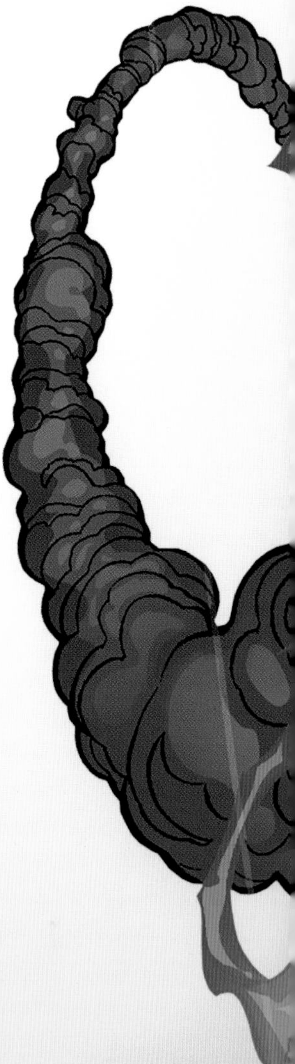

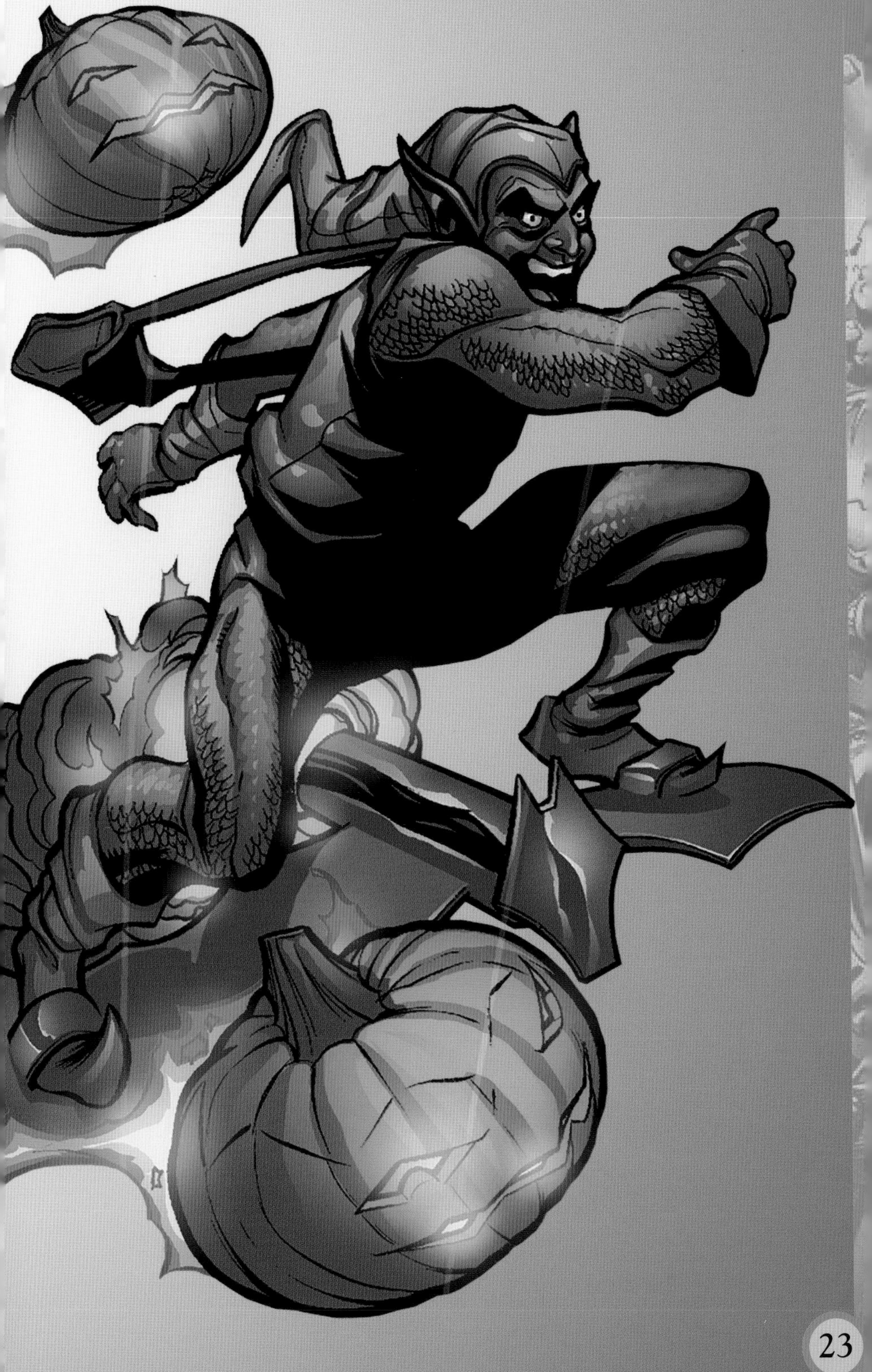

Kang

Kang the Conqueror is a human from the distant future. He uses a time machine to travel through time and space. This villain wants to conquer all the worlds across the universe.

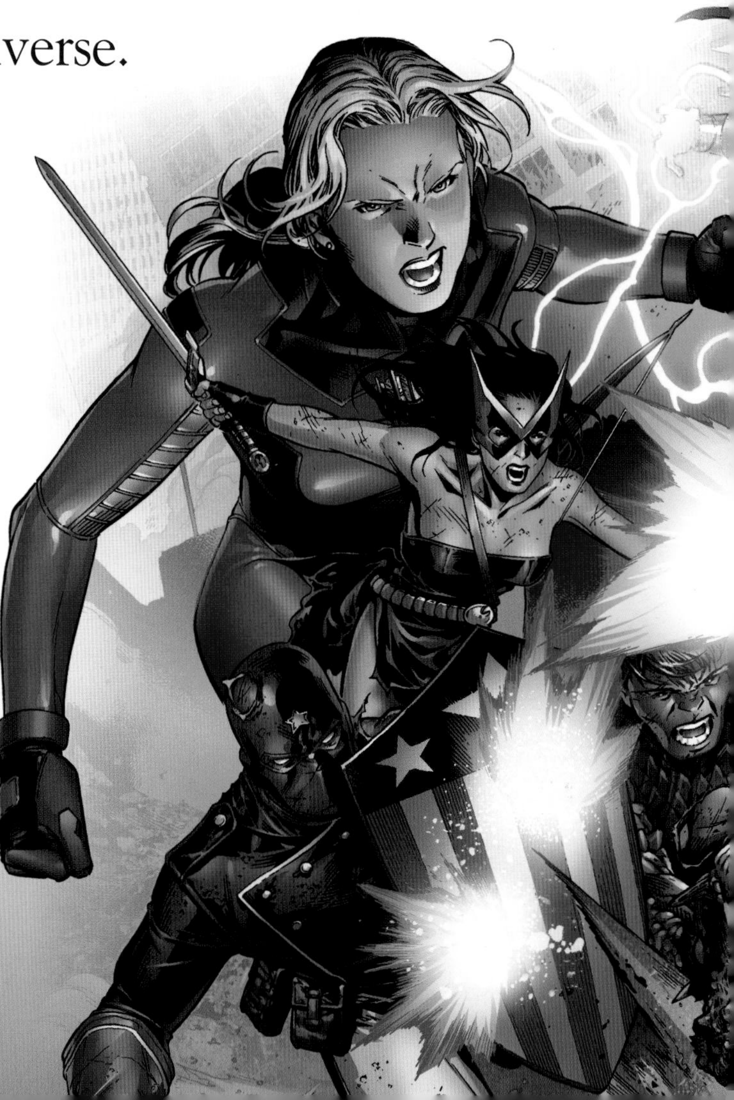

Kang's intelligence, futuristic armor, and hi-tech weapons make him a fearsome foe. Even the Avengers find him hard to beat!

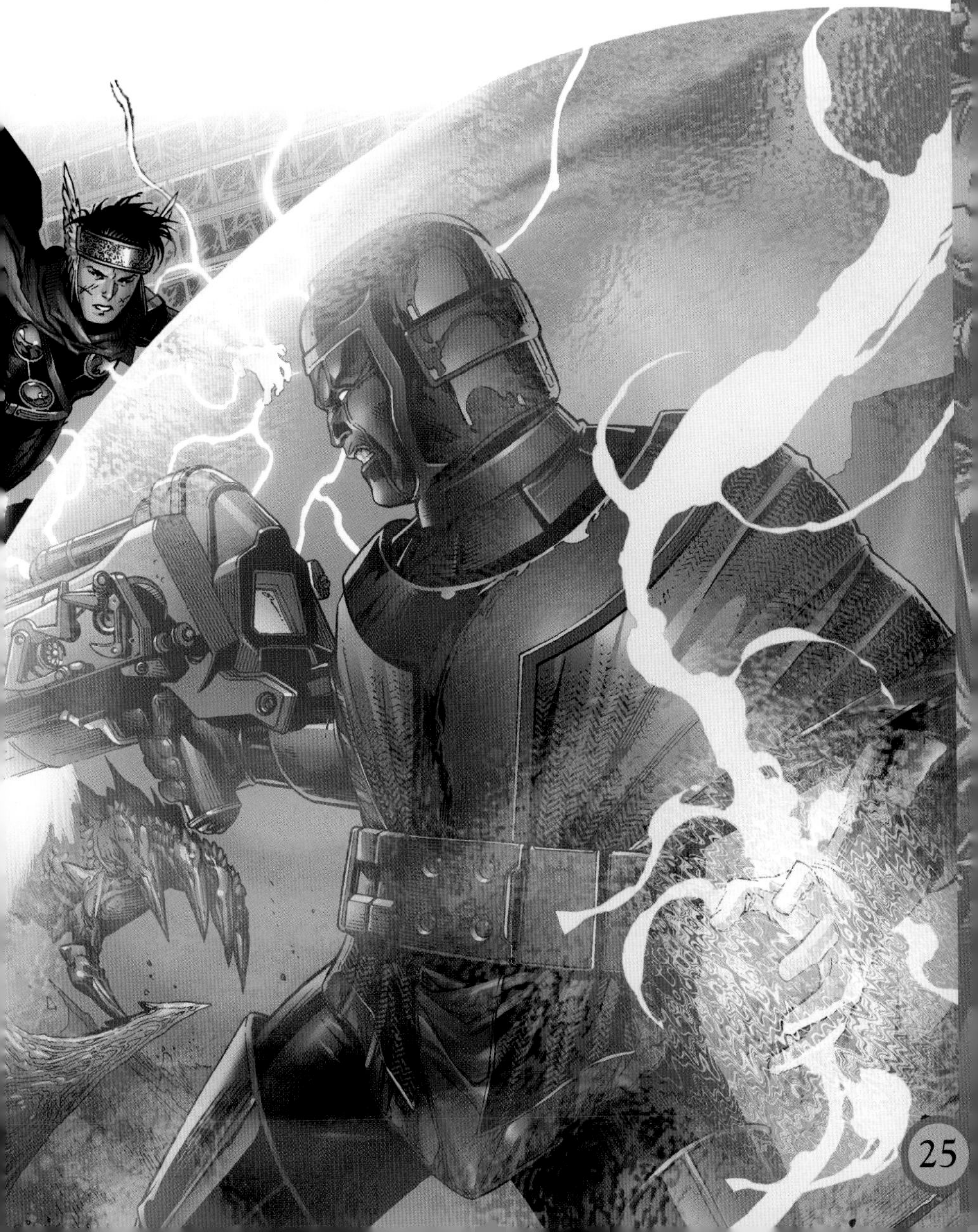

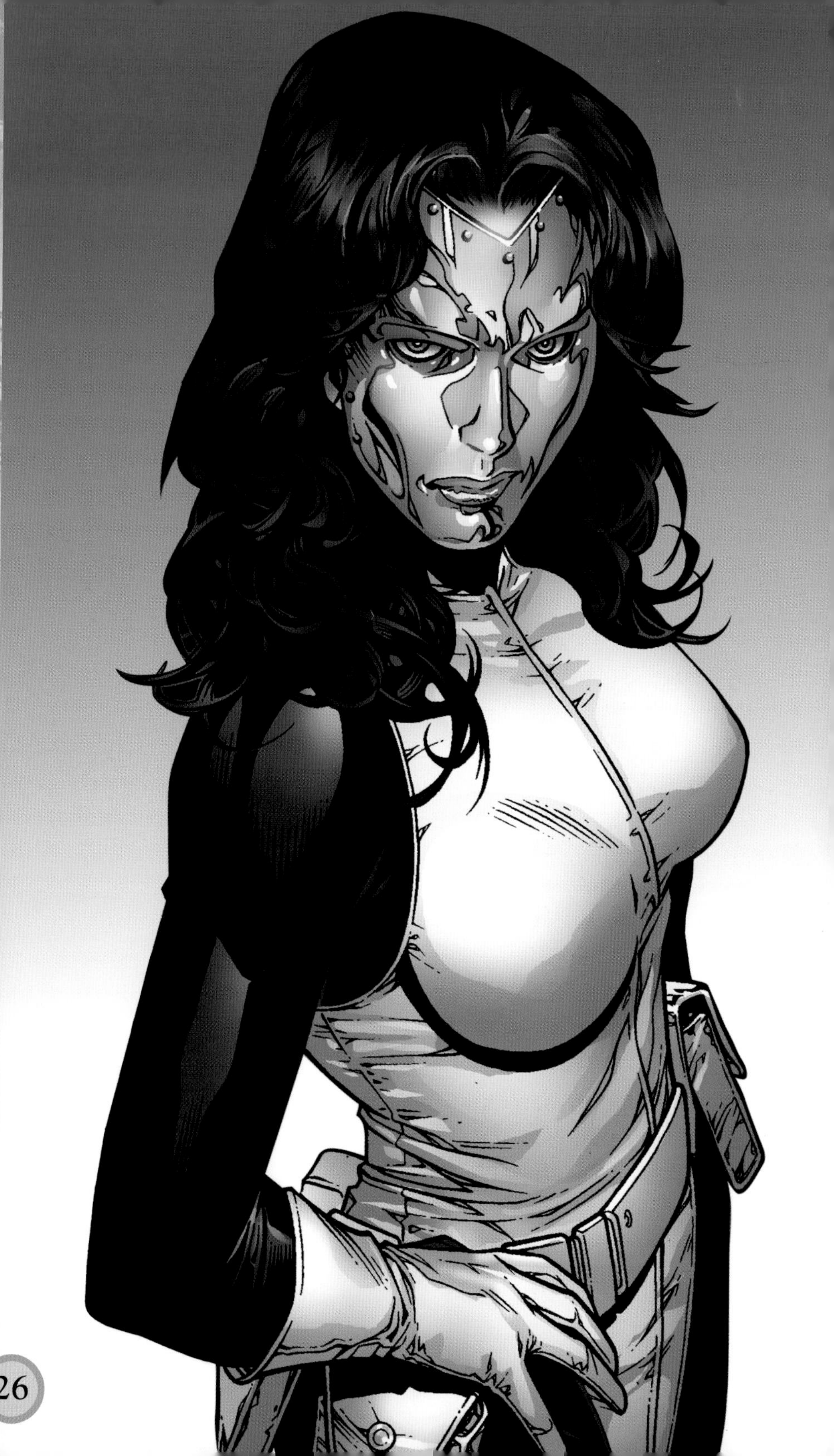

Madame Masque

Madame Masque often fights the Super Hero Iron Man. She is the leader of the criminal group known as the Maggia.

Madame Masque is smart, sneaky, and deadly. Her gold mask hides scars that she received in a terrible accident. She is very good at disguising herself as other people.

Dormammu

Dormammu is an
all-powerful being
made of mystic energy.
He is the fiery lord
of a strange realm
known as the
Dark Dimension.

Dormammu seeks to rule all
the dimensions in the universe.
He is always stopped by
Doctor Strange, the strongest
sorcerer on Earth.

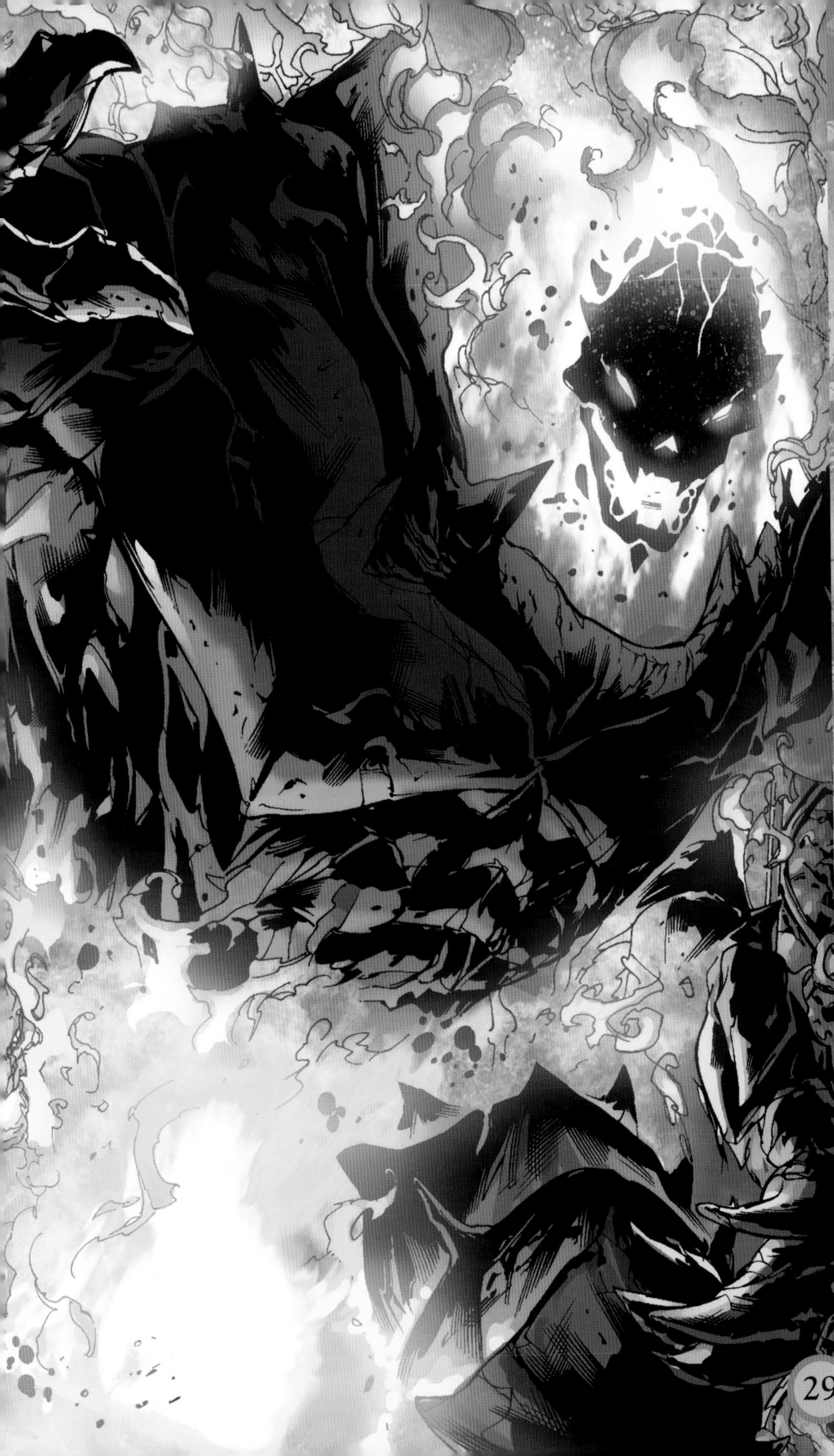

CRIMINAL LOCATIONS

Villains need kingdoms and bases where they can make evil plans. If these crooks are caught by brave heroes, they are locked up in super-secure prisons!

Hel

Hela controls Hel, the land of the dead. She can change the landscape with just her mind.

The Big House

This prison is named the Big House, but it is actually tiny! Scientist Hank Pym shrinks criminals down to very small sizes, so they can fit inside.

Oscorp Tower

Oscorp is the Green Goblin's company. The company is based at the Oscorp Tower. All of the villain's technology is made here.

Dark Dimension

This creepy dimension is enormous! The worlds that Dormammu rules are kept here. He adds to his collection all the time.

The Kyln

Criminals beware, the Kyln is a Super Villain prison! These ball-shaped jail cells can be found in outer space.

Abomination

This reptile-like monster was once a human. He was transformed into a scaly creature by the same gamma radiation that created the Super Hero Hulk.

Abomination is as mean as he is ugly. This villain wants to prove he is stronger than Hulk, but he never succeeds.

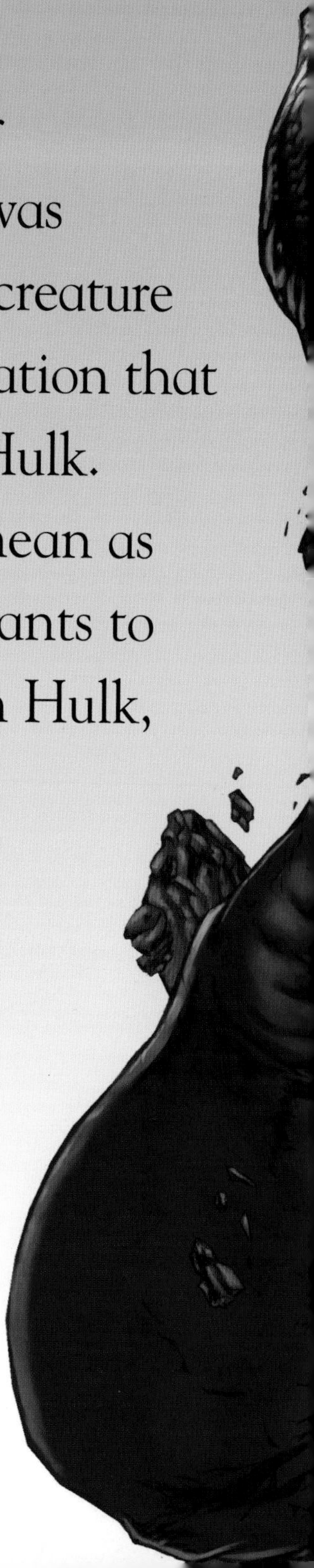

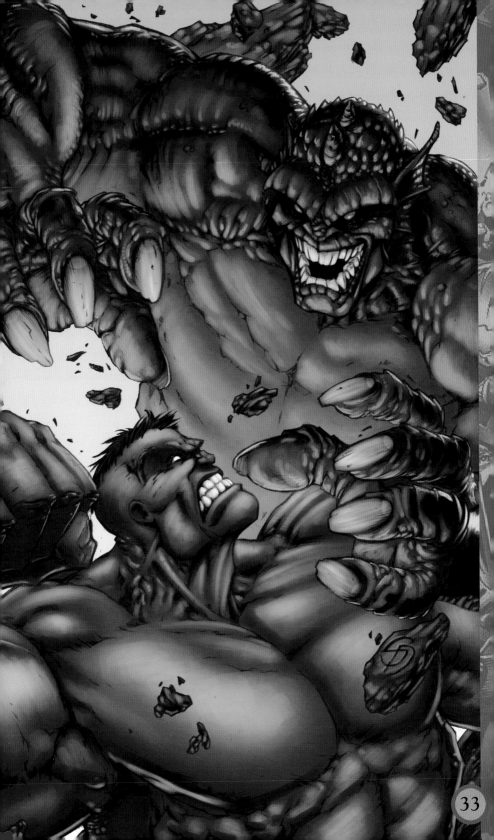

M.O.D.O.K.

M.O.D.O.K. is a mad scientist who wants to rule the world. He is part-man, part-computer. This odd-looking Super Villain uses a hover-chair to move, because his huge head makes walking very difficult.

M.O.D.O.K. is always scheming against Super Heroes like Captain America and Hulk. Fortunately, he always loses!

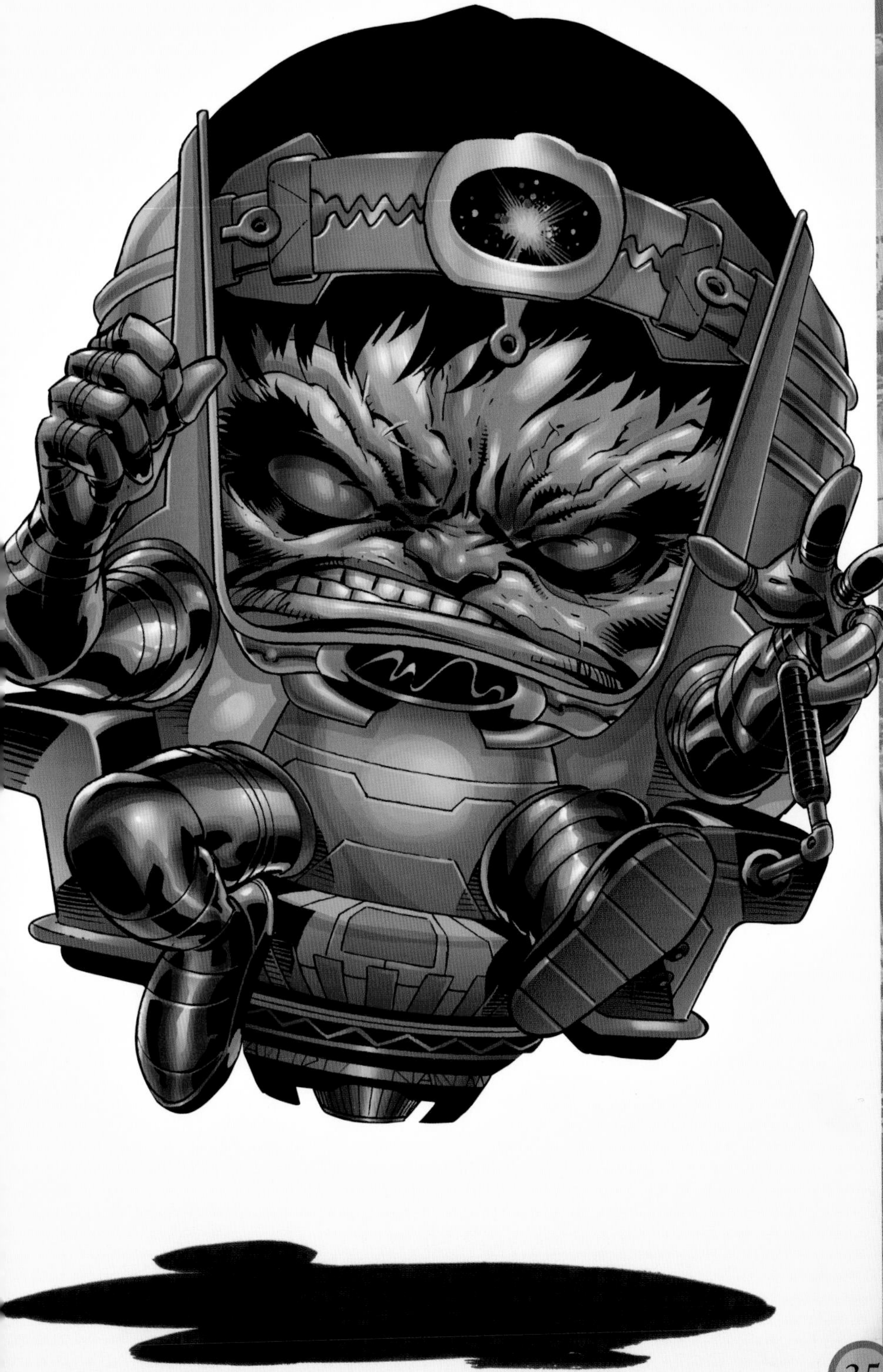

Enchantress

Enchantress is a wicked and powerful goddess from Asgard. She has great magical skills and superhuman strength.

Enchantress longs to rule over the kingdom of Asgard with the Avenger Thor by her side. She tries to use magic to win him over, but he is able to resist her spells.

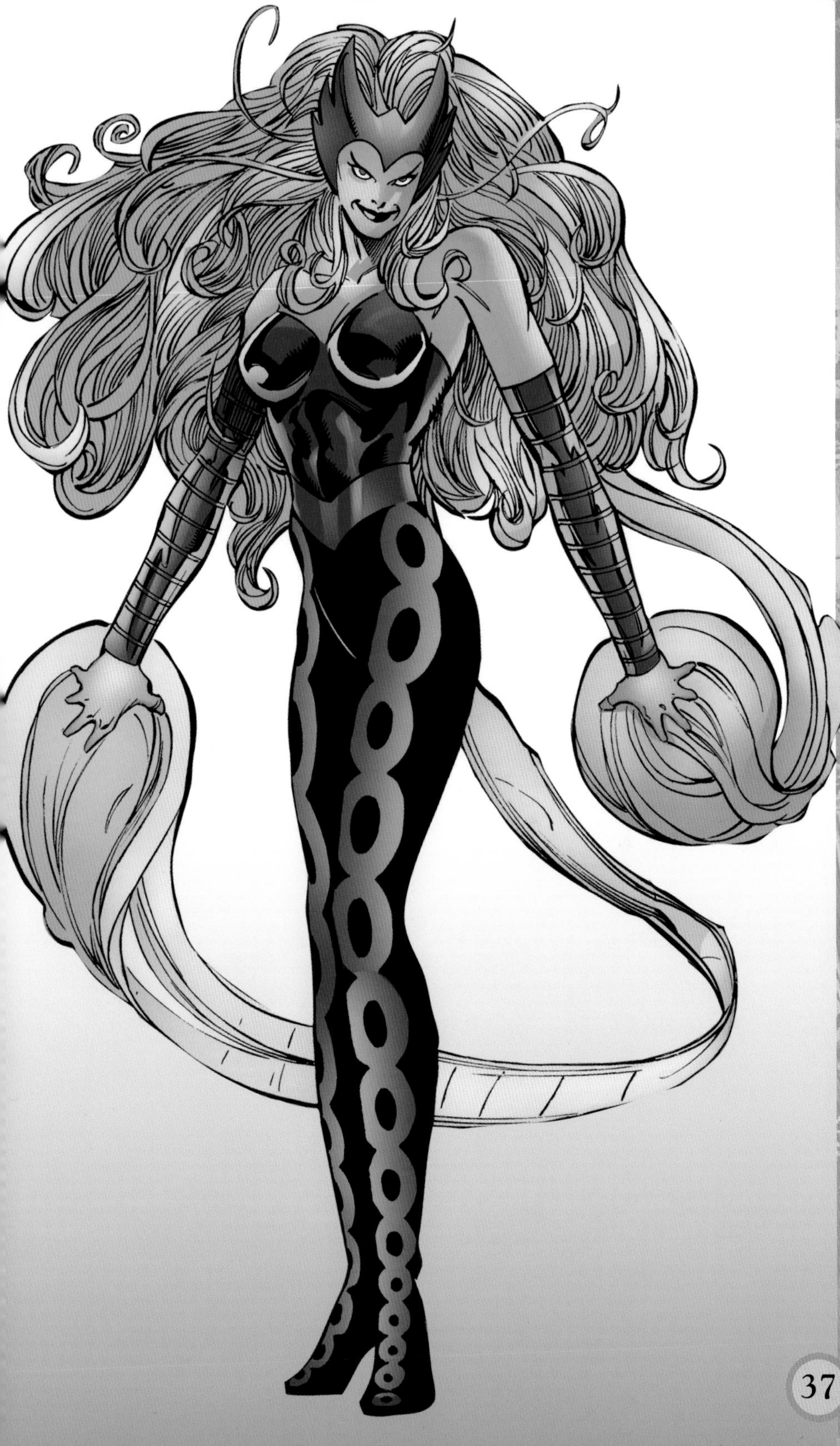

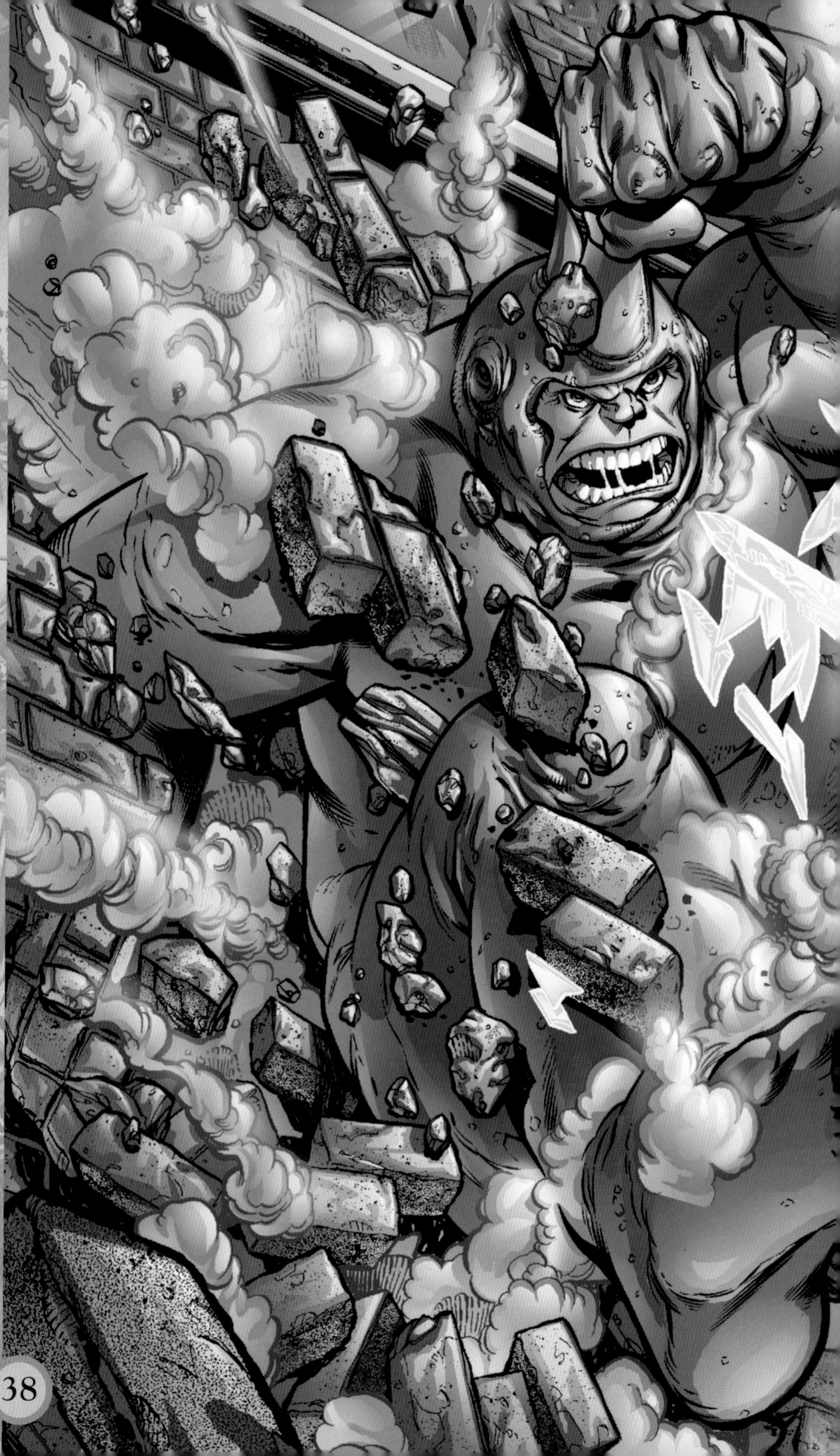

Rhino

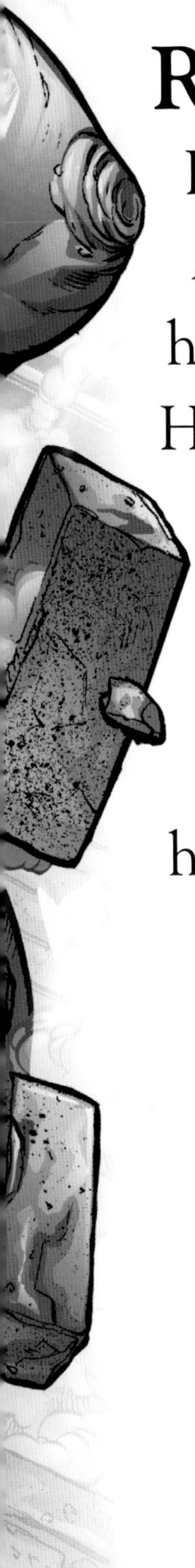

Rhino is a superhuman villain. A pair of scientists created him during an experiment. He has rhinoceros-like skin and steel-piercing horns. Rhino is a fierce fighter, and often battles Spider-Man and Hulk. Fortunately for the heroes, he is not very smart.

Ulysses Klaw

This Super Villain is made
of sonic energy. Klaw replaces
one of his hands for a
powerful sonic blaster.

Klaw was once an assassin.
He killed T'Chaka, the King
of Wakanda. T'Chaka was
also a Super Hero, named
Black Panther. T'Chaka's son,
T'Challa, became the new
Black Panther. Now T'Challa
hunts Klaw for revenge.

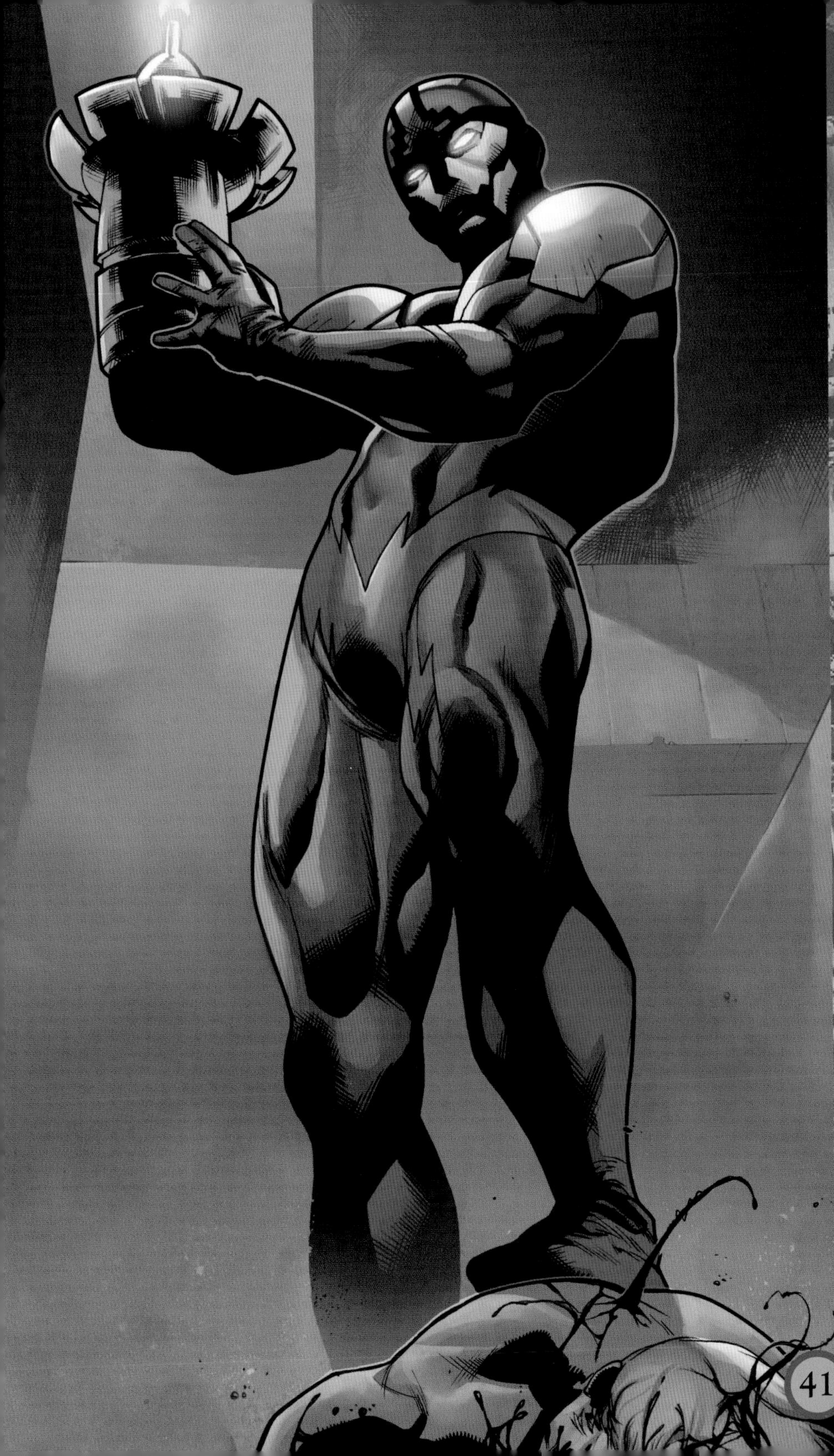

AWESOME OBJECTS

There are many strange and powerful items to help villains defeat annoying heroes. With magic, or other forces, these devices could destroy the world!

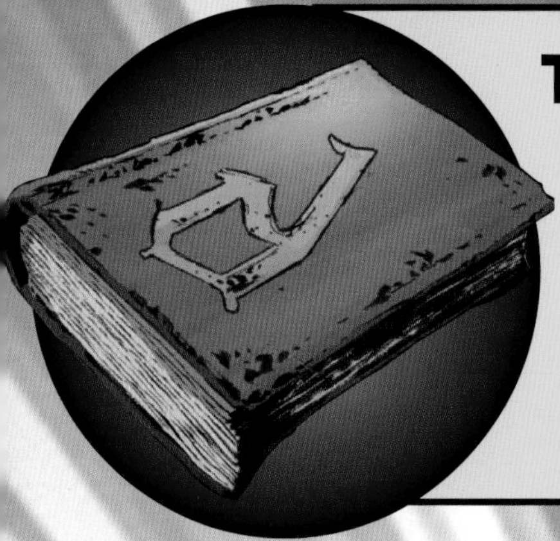

The *Darkhold*

This mysterious book contains many horrible spells. Inside, there are spells for unleashing werewolves and vampires.

Cosmic Cube

The owner of a Cosmic Cube has the power to change reality. It is hard to make a cube, but Red Skull succeeds.

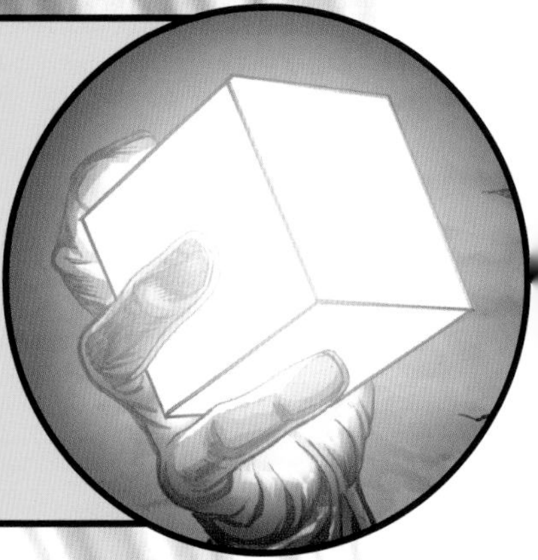